This journal belongs to

....

Date ....

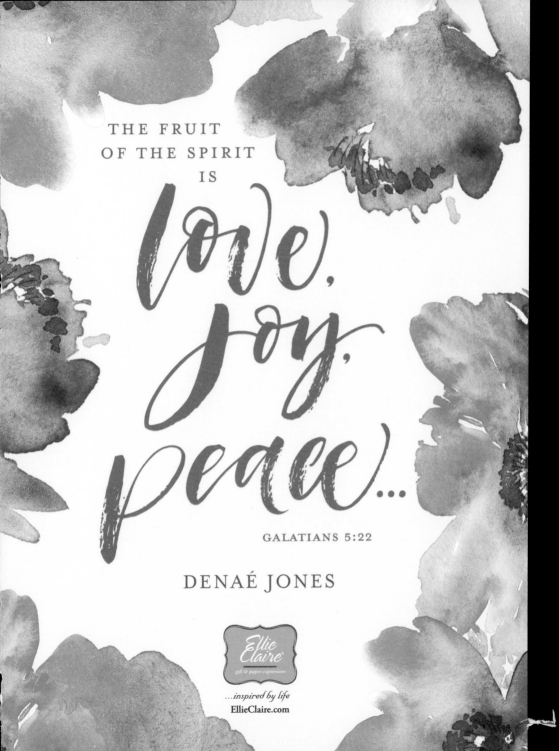

THE FRUIT
OF THE SPIRIT
IS

love,

joy,

peace...

GALATIANS 5:22

DENAÉ JONES

Ellie Claire®

gift & paper expressions

...*inspired by life*
EllieClaire.com

Ellie Claire® Gift & Paper Expressions
Franklin, TN 37067
EllieClaire.com
Ellie Claire is a registered trademark of Worthy Media, Inc.

Love, Joy, Peace...
© 2017 by Denaé Jones
Published by Ellie Claire, an imprint of Worthy Publishing Group, a division of Worthy Media, Inc.

ISBN 978-1-63326-167-9

Unless otherwise noted, all Scripture quotations are taken from: The Holy Bible, New International Version®, NIV® Copyright © 1973, 1978, 1984, 2011 by Biblica, Inc.® All rights reserved worldwide. Other Scripture from: The New American Standard Bible® (NASB), Copyright © 1960, 1962, 1963, 1968, 1971, 1972, 1973, 1975, 1977, 1995 by The Lockman Foundation. The Holy Bible, English Standard Version® (ESV®), copyright © 2001 by Crossway Bibles, a publishing ministry of Good News Publishers. The Holy Bible, New Living Translation (NLT) copyright © 1996, 2004, 2007 by Tyndale House Foundation. Used by permission of Tyndale House Publishers Inc., Carol Stream, Illinois 60188.

Stock or custom editions of Ellie Claire titles may be purchased in bulk for educational, business, ministry, fundraising, or sales promotional use. For information, please e-mail info@EllieClaire.com

Cover design by Melissa Reagan
Interior design by Jeff Jansen | aestheticsoup.net
Art by shutterstock.com
Lettering by istockphoto.com

Printed in China.

1 2 3 4 5 6 7 8 9 –RRD– 21 20 19 18 17

The fruit of the Spirit is love,

joy, peace, patience, kindness,

goodness, faithfulness,

gentleness, self-control;

against such things there is no law.

GALATIANS 5:22–23 NASB

Introduction

Love, joy, peace, patience, kindness, goodness, faithfulness, gentleness, and self-control. We read about this fruit of the Holy Spirit in the Bible, but what does it really look like? How do we apply it to our late-for-a-meeting, burned-dinner, kids-are-fighting, boss-is-nagging, I-need-a-vacation lives today? In this book, we will explore how the fruit of the spirit is a living, breathing part of our day-to-day existence.

It is called fruit because it has to grow. It is not something we create on our own, but rather something that is nurtured and strengthened within us when we surrender to God.

It is our hope that these devotions will help you do just that. Journaling lines are provided where you can reflect on how each fruit is evident in your own life and record steps you can take to help that fruit continue to grow.

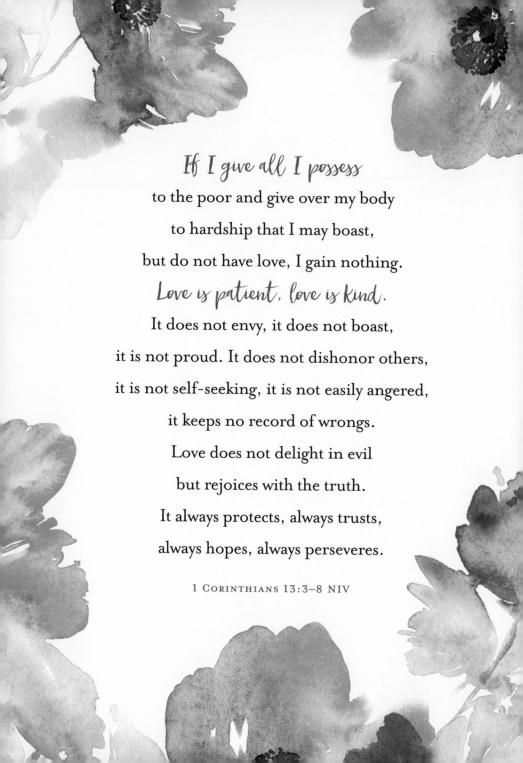

If I give all I possess

to the poor and give over my body

to hardship that I may boast,

but do not have love, I gain nothing.

Love is patient, love is kind.

It does not envy, it does not boast,

it is not proud. It does not dishonor others,

it is not self-seeking, it is not easily angered,

it keeps no record of wrongs.

Love does not delight in evil

but rejoices with the truth.

It always protects, always trusts,

always hopes, always perseveres.

1 Corinthians 13:3–8 NIV

Where Did the Time Go?

See what great love the Father has lavished on us,
that we should be called children of God! And that is what we are!
The reason the world does not know us is that it did not know him.

1 JOHN 3:1

I love to do things every once in a while to catch my kids totally by surprise. One day at the end of October it was abnormally hot, and we got an unexpected pop-up thunderstorm. When I looked out the upstairs window, our three youngest children were standing in the front yard. Their mouths were open in disbelief, their arms up. They weren't sure whether to run for cover or not. I ran downstairs and opened the front door. All eyes were on me, expecting me to yell at them for being outside in their clothes. By that time, it was an absolute downpour, but instead of making them come in, I took off my socks and ran outside with them. The kids looked at each other with the same shock as when the downpour came out of nowhere. They squealed with delight, "Mommy is running in the rain!" and ran over to me. We danced and skipped and spun in circles and had races. We screamed and laughed and got muddy and had the time of our lives. As an added bonus, we were blessed with a fantastic double rainbow stretching over the sky. It was a great day.

I am so glad that I chose to run outside that day instead of continuing my household chores. If you are a parent, you know that we are often faced with showing our kids how much we love them by enforcing discipline. We love them too much to let them continue displaying an unpleasant behavior. Unfortunately, they don't usually understand that kind of love until they are much older. However, this day my kids got to see my love for them dance itself through the front yard, as I remembered how much fun it was being a kid.

At the same time, it made me a little sad. I realized that it shouldn't be a shock to them that I would take part in such spontaneity. I used to do stuff like that all the time. When did it stop? My kids won't want to do things like that with me forever, and I had wasted so much time sitting out because I was too tired. Or didn't have time. Or didn't want to get my clothes dirty. Or wanted to sit and have an adult conversation instead. Yes, I certainly need those things sometimes, but it was suddenly so evident to me that I will be an adult forever and they will only be kids once.

We have a thousand opportunities every day to create memorable moments. This week, I challenge you to be creative with how you spend your time. Think outside the box and do something fun. I challenge you to walk away from the distractions of your phone or television and do something more meaningful with the people you love. I challenge you to spend your time in a way that makes you smile simply because you know it's making God smile. Talk with God and let Him know how much you love Him too. It feels so nice to go to bed at night and think, "Yes. That was a really good day."

Thank You, Father God, for giving me child-like joy in unexpected and wonderful ways. May I never miss a rainbow or sunset because I am too busy to notice. Help me to love You and others more completely.

Mirror Messages

Dear friends, let us love one another, for love comes from God.
Everyone who loves has been born of God and knows God.
1 JOHN 4:7

Being a mother of six, I have days when I sneak into another room to hide, just to try and find five minutes to myself. Since my closet is conveniently located in our bathroom, I may have been known to lock myself in and eat the good Halloween candy I stashed away when nobody was looking. They call it being sneaky. I call it keeping my sanity. That's what I was doing awhile back when I noticed something really cool. You know how, if someone writes on your fogged-up car window with their finger, the message seems to keep reappearing? That's what happens on my bathroom mirror every time it gets steamed up from a shower. Messages that have long since been wiped off find their way to the surface again, and they always make me smile.

You see, a year or so ago my husband unknowingly started a family tradition when he started leaving me sweet messages on our bathroom mirror, written with a dry erase marker. Every day there would be a new one, and every day I would look forward to coming home to see what my new mirror message would say. So I started sneaking in to write mirror messages for him to see when he got up for work. Eventually we would go in to get ready for bed and see a message the kids had left for us. Now it's common to see "I love you Mom!" or "I will miss you while I'm gone," or to find a carefully drawn picture of all of us holding hands.

After a while, the messages crept from my bathroom mirror to the mirrors in the other bathrooms. I would leave them messages like "Be God's light to someone today. It might be the only light they see." The next week it might say, "Do three acts of kindness today and don't tell anyone what they are." My hope is that they will read it while they stand there and brush their teeth and that it will make a small difference in their actions that day. Maybe it will help them be a better friend. Maybe it will help them realize their worth. Maybe it will help them think about the good that can come out of even the worst days. Maybe their lovingkindness will make a difference in someone else's life too.

So now when I sneak in and hide in the bathroom closet to eat my chocolate (where I don't have to split one bite-size candy bar into eight pieces), I can sometimes catch a glimpse of those old messages that had been previously erased. Messages of love. Encouragement. Messages just to let someone know they were being thought about. We stuck a few markers in a cup next to the bathroom sink and I have loved watching what unfolds. I encourage you to do the same.

Lord, I thank You for the unexpected reminders of love that surround me every day. I thank You for loving me unconditionally. Even when I feel unlovely. Even when I feel I don't deserve it. Even if, at times, my actions don't show that I love You back, You love me anyway. Help me to never take that love for granted. Help me to do the same for others.

Boxes Full of Memories

*However, as it is written: "What no eye has seen,
what no ear has heard, and what no human mind has conceived"—
the things God has prepared for those who love him.*
1 Corinthians 2:9

My little one tiptoed into my room, crawled under the blankets, and snuggled in the "nook" of my arm this morning. She kissed my cheek and whispered, "I love you, Mama," before she dozed off again. She was safe and warm and loved, and all was right in her world. I cherish those moments.

When it was time to get the others up for school, I paused beside their beds before I woke them. I wanted to breathe in the innocence of their childhood and take a snapshot in my mind of how sweet and little and happy they looked, snuggled safe in their beds. I didn't want to wake them, because I knew that in a few moments I would have to give them news that would take a little bit of that innocence away. I would have to tell them that their beloved great-grandmother had passed away. I would have to prepare them for the heartache of another funeral. They have lost two grandparents and three great-grandparents in two years, as well as other relatives and friends. That is more heartache than a child should have to bear. I didn't want to tell them yet again that a part of their lives would change forever. The mama in me wanted to hold them all in the nook of my arms and keep them safe from all of the sadness. But it just doesn't work that way.

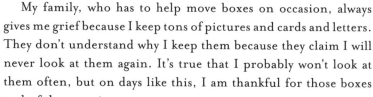 My family, who has to help move boxes on occasion, always gives me grief because I keep tons of pictures and cards and letters. They don't understand why I keep them because they claim I will never look at them again. It's true that I probably won't look at them often, but on days like this, I am thankful for those boxes full of wonderful memories.

Today I will pull out boxed items for my kids to look at from their great-grandmother. As they get older, they will eventually understand that the boxes they hate to move contain their precious cargo too. Today the pictures from those boxes will bring back happy memories to make them smile. Today the cards in those boxes will help them remember that she never forgot their birthdays. Today the news of her passing will make them cry, but we won't focus on her death. Today, as we rejoice in the fact that this is the first day of her life in heaven, the contents of those boxes will help them rejoice in her life well-lived with them here. Life is so fleeting, and sometimes it's really difficult. But wow! It's so amazing too. Think of the most awesome thing you have ever seen. Isn't it fascinating to think that God prepared things even more awesome than that for us in heaven? Our human minds cannot even conceive it. God love us so!

I encourage you to become your family historian. Take lots of pictures, and date them. Write things down. Break out the video camera more often. Capture the awe of the great parts of your life. Talk more. Hug longer. Let them know how much they are loved.

Dear Jesus, sometimes I wonder how You could love me enough to die for me. I have let You down so many times. Then I look into the eyes of my family and dearest friends. I love them so much that I feel my heart could burst. And then I remember that I am Your child. That is how You feel when You look at me. Thank You, gracious God, for loving me in my brokenness. Help me to love others in theirs.

The Spirit of Love

There are many memes that read "Love is…" However, the endings are all different. Some think love is finding their soulmate. Some think love is making sacrifices for others. Some think love is eating a giant cheeseburger. Some have no idea how to finish that sentence.

Thankfully, Scripture gives us hundreds of examples of what love is, *who* we are to love, and *how* we are to love. Jesus told us in Matthew 22:37–39 to "'love the Lord your God with all your heart and with all your soul and with all your mind.' This is the first and greatest commandment. And the second is like it: 'Love your neighbor as yourself.'" We are even told to love our enemies. Sometimes that seems impossible, until we remember that we are made in the image and likeness of God (Genesis 1:27). And *God is love* (1 John 4:8).

Friends, if God is love, and we are created like Him, we are created *from* love, and we are created *to* love. God loves us when we deserve it, and when we don't, because love is the very essence of His being. First John 3:16 says, "This is how we know what love is: Jesus Christ laid down his life for us." Amen!

So how can we finish that sentence? Easy. "Love is…*God*."

What steps can we take to accept God's love more completely? How can we demonstrate it to others?

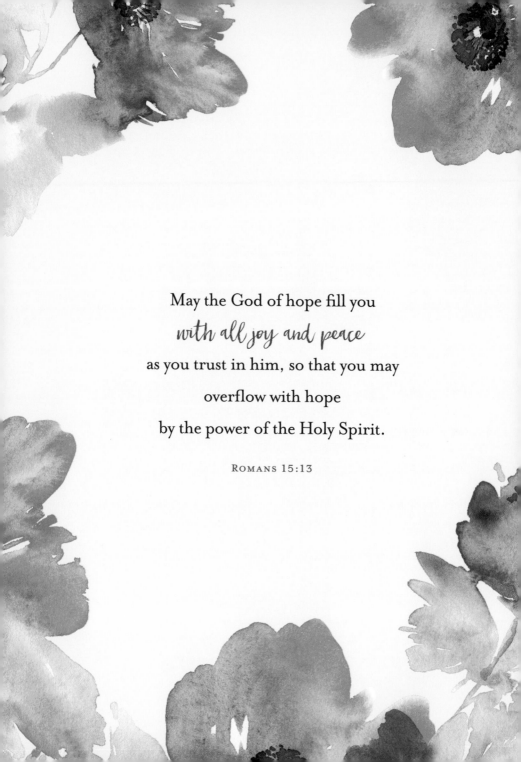

May the God of hope fill you

with all joy and peace

as you trust in him, so that you may

overflow with hope

by the power of the Holy Spirit.

ROMANS 15:13

Live, Love, and Laugh at Yourself

Our mouths were filled with laughter, our tongues with songs of joy.
Then it was said among the nations,
"The LORD has done great things for them."
The LORD has done great things for us, and we are filled with joy.
PSALM 126:2–3

Sometime in the late eighties to early nineties, baby doll dresses were in style. They were kind of short and flowy, and I had a couple that I loved and wore to work. At that time, I was working in an office, and one summer day I volunteered to take orders and get everyone some ice cream. I underestimated the number of hands it would take to complete this task. Once I had everything back to the office parking lot, I contemplated making two trips to bring it all in, but the car was really hot and I knew the ice cream would be melted if I had to come back for any of it. So I decided I was smart enough to figure out how to do it in one trip.

I got out of my car, locked the door with my elbow, held my keyring in my mouth, purse on my shoulder, one ice cream cone in my left hand, and leaned in to grab the holder with the rest of the ice cream cups. It was all going as planned until I backed out of the car and pushed the locked door shut with my knee, because that is exactly when a big breeze blew. It flipped the back of my dress up over my head at exactly the instant the locked door slammed shut...with my dress stuck in the top of it. Yep. That's a bit of a predicament.

As if it wasn't embarrassing enough that the dress blew up, the fact that it was stuck over my head in a locked door, essentially pinning me to the car, was downright humiliating. It was going to take me a minute to figure out how to get out of this mess. I had to put down the ice cream without spilling anything, find the right key, unlock the door, get my dress out, and pick everything back up. Somehow, I did it.

Then I did what anyone would do. I stood tall as if nothing had happened and didn't dare look around for fear of making eye contact with anyone who could have seen what just unfolded. I walked into the office, gave everyone their ice cream, and sat down. It got really quiet. Then I broke out in uncontrollable laughter. The kind of laughter that brings tears. It was at my own expense, but it just would not stop. It took awhile for me to compose myself enough to tell the girls what had happened because I was laughing so hard I couldn't speak.

Something changed in me that day. Maybe it's because I was utterly humiliated and realized that I lived through it. It gave me a strange sense of confidence that I was lacking before. As a teenager, I thought people would like me less if they saw my flaws. And doesn't that sometimes carry over to adulthood? That's such an exhausting way to live. Everyone has flaws. Even those who criticize you for yours. Don't be so hard on yourself today. Choose joy!

Thank You, God, for the gift of laugher. It is such a wonderful sound! Help me to always be able to find the deep belly laugh kind of joy that can only come from You.

Where Did the Time Go?

I thank my God every time I remember you.
In all my prayers for all of you, I always pray with joy.
PHILIPPIANS 1:3–4

Many people think happiness and joy are the same thing. They aren't. Happiness is a feeling. Joy is a choice. We can feel happy when our favorite song comes on the radio, but as soon as it's over, that feeling of happiness might go away. That fleeting feeling is not enough to sustain us through the difficult times. But joy is different. It has to come from within, and it doesn't always come easily. Sometimes we find ourselves deep in despair but then see a glimmer of hope. When we choose to grab onto that hope and hang on for dear life, we choose joy. When our broken heart finds peace, we choose joy. When we choose to let go of the negative and look for the blessings, we choose joy. When we cry "happy tears," it is because we have chosen joy.

Time is precious, friends, and we have to guard it carefully. There are many songs that say we don't know when our last time is going to be our last time. It's so true. The reality often hits when we see the empty chair of a loved one for the first time. The silence is deafening. It's hard to be joyful when a part of you is missing. It's hard to celebrate when you really just want to be alone. It's hard to smile when you want to cry.

A friend of mine posted something that I want to share with you:

Getting ready to set up the Christmas tree this morning, and contemplating the holidays without two very precious members of the family. Then it occurs to me that Dad and Joe have actually given me a beautiful gift this year—the gift of renewed, genuine love and appreciation for the amazing family and friends I am blessed to have! I will choose to celebrate the ones I love rather than mourn what I have lost. Rather than just surviving this holiday season—I choose to celebrate! I'm certain there will be tears, but I am determined there will also be joy. Thank you, Dad and Joe, for the early gift this year! (...but still love and miss you both like crazy).

Our loved ones wouldn't want us to cry over the empty seats. They would want us to have joy. I encourage you to give the gift of your time to someone today. Time to listen. Time to talk. Time to plan that road trip you've been talking about. Time to work on that project together. Maybe even time to run in the rain. When the day comes that the empty chair at the table is the one you used to sit in, the family and friends still sitting there probably won't remember what gift you gave them at Christmas. But they will always remember the time you spent together, and that will give them joy for years to come.

Friend, if you are struggling with grief today, I ask you to think about what you wish others would do for you. Then use that to help another grieving person find joy. Sometimes it's enough to simply say, "I was thinking about [name] today and it made me smile. I thought you would like to know."

Dear heavenly Father, sometimes choosing joy seems like an impossible task. Thank You for showing me that nothing is impossible when I put my trust in You. Thank You for taking my broken pieces and making them whole again. Help me to always choose joy.

Moments

When anxiety was great within me, your consolation brought me joy.
PSALM 94:19

It was my five-year-old's first time riding her bike with no training wheels down the road with all of us.

I said: "Stay by me! Keep over to the side! Don't get too close to the bike in front of you. Don't get too far in front of everyone else. Watch for cars! Watch for dogs! Don't go too fast! Check your brakes. Slow down!"

She said: "I know how to do it. You're not being fun. I can go fast like everyone else! I know how to watch for cars. I might be YOUR baby, but I'm NOT a baby anymore! *I'm not a baby anymore.*"

So I backed off and put my little girl in God's hands. I clung to the back and let her go.... And she flew! Pigtails flying, legs alternating between pedaling as fast as they would go and then being thrown out to the side as she soared down the hill. For her five-year-old little heart, that's what freedom looked like. She didn't crash. She watched for cars. She kept up with all the boys. She had FUN! It was a reality check that she is growing up and becoming more independent, and I needed to let her. *I cannot let my anxiety be what inhibits her joy,* I told myself.

Wasn't it just yesterday that she was afraid to get on the bike with no training wheels? And hadn't I been right there with her brothers and sisters, encouraging her over and over to face her fears and hop back on and try again? So why did her small victory to conquer a "big girl bike" bring a twinge of sadness to my mama heart? That's when I realized that this bike ride was one of *those* moments. You know the kind I'm talking about. The kind of moment when something happens that ends a chapter in someone's life and opens a new one.

I looked around the garage and realized that the two wheeled bikes had taken the place of the little plastic pedal bikes. Nobody had ridden them in a long time. Then it dawned on me that they probably never will again. When did that happen? In this case, I guess it happened the moment my youngest asked to go on that bike ride with us and I said yes. Just that quickly, a part of her childhood was left behind. It will be filed away with the memories of her pacifiers, Pull-Ups, and footed jammies that all slipped through the cracks when I wasn't looking. Time sure does fly. And given the chance to soar, so do little pigtails on a five-year-old without training wheels. It was a bittersweet day, but God's consolation made my heart joyful as I laid my anxiety down and witnessed her small victory.

Today I challenge you to reflect on what kind of special "moments" you are creating with your family and friends. If you aren't sure, make plans to create some. It could be something as simple as sitting on the porch swing together and talking about the events of your day. Or playing a board game, or taking a walk. Just have a few laughs over favorite memories. It doesn't have to be extravagant to be memorable.

Dear heavenly Father, thank You for holding me steady when my knees are weak. Thank You for showing me that the joy that comes from You is much bigger than any anxiety I create. Help me to replace my stress and fear with joy that can only come from You.

Feel the Joy

My mom is one of those people who makes you feel like you are important every time she talks to you. It doesn't matter if you are a lifelong friend, a stranger, or a client at her work; she greets everyone with equal enthusiasm. When we were kids and living at home, she would give us a huge smile and cheerful "Good morning!" every day. Even when we were grumpy. Even when we were grounded. Even when we had hurt her feelings. I remember wondering *how* someone could be that happy to see me all the time.

Then I had a family of my own and I totally understood. My eyes light up and my heart smiles when I see each one of them. Even when they are grumpy, or grounded, or have hurt my feelings. I finally understood that it isn't just happiness that my mom shows everyone. It's *joy*. It doesn't come from circumstance, it comes from within. How exciting it is to think that God, who is our Father, feels joy when He looks at us!

Psalm 16:11 says, "You make known to me the path of life; *you will fill me with joy in your presence*" (emphasis added). Let's take time each day to stand in the presence of God and ask Him to direct our path of life. Let us feel the joy of His faithful and loving Spirit.

How can you spread joy in your corner of the world today?

Peace I leave with you;

my peace I give you.

I do not give to you as the world gives.

Do not let your hearts be troubled

and do not be afraid.

JOHN 14:27

Let's All Retire... Right Now!

Do not be anxious about anything, but in every situation,
by prayer and petition, with thanksgiving, present your requests to God.
And the peace of God, which transcends all understanding,
will guard your hearts and your minds in Christ Jesus.
PHILIPPIANS 4:6–7

One day a friend posted, "We have decided something big! We have decided to retire." They are my age. (Which I try to tell myself is really young.) How in the world could they be retiring already? Then I read on. "We are retiring the negativity. We are retiring the despair. We are retiring the hopelessness. We are retiring the doubt that has infested our home. We have a retirement plan in place and can't wait to begin!" That may very well be the best retirement plan I've heard of yet.

As I lay in bed and replayed all of the negativity of the day in my mind, I realized there was way too much of it. I felt like it was one of those days when I totally bombed as a parent. I was thankful that, God willing, a new day was just hours away and I could try again. I decided to make my own "retirement" plan.

How could I retire negativity? With kindness. I want to use more kind words. Sometimes I'm quick to point out what others have done wrong but don't tell them often enough what they've done right. It takes the same amount of time to do both. This week I'm going to strive to show more kindness to myself and to others. I'm going to give more compliments and be more encouraging.

How could I retire despair? With joy. Children are the best teachers when it comes to finding joy in the little things. When was the last time you sang a silly song, just for fun? And it's surprising how much joy there is in taking a child's hand and skipping with them, without caring who is watching. This week I am going to strive to step outside of my grown-up mind and look for that child-like joy.

How could I retire hopelessness? With peace. Having a peaceful moment is not the same as having peace. On a day-to-day basis, we are dealing with running late, forgotten lunches, bickering, burned dinners, sickness, pain, and sometimes even death. But when we can experience those things and still feel calm in our hearts and minds, that is peace. People find peace in a lot of different ways. I find mine when I pray. In prayer, I used to do all of the talking. Over time, I learned that sometimes I need to just be quiet and listen. This week I am going to strive to make more time to just "be" with God and let His peace soak in.

How can I retire doubt? With faithfulness. I have a difficult time putting certain jobs in the hands of others. I have doubt that they will get done the "right" way. I've learned that, even though the dishwasher is not stacked the way I would have done it, it's still stacked, and I didn't have to do it. This week I will strive to put more faith in others. I will try to put more faith in God and let His grace in those situations be sufficient. This week I will strive to have more faith in myself. I realize this won't happen overnight, and I will still mess up. A lot. But I'm certain it's the only surefire way to get "rich" quick.

Dear Lord, sometimes there is so much going on that I cannot find peace. Help me to hear Your voice in the chaos. Create in me a peace that surpasses all understanding.

Thank You for Being a Friend

But it is you, a man like myself, my companion,
my close friend, whom I once enjoyed
the sweet fellowship at the house of God,
as we walked about among the worshipers.
PSALM 55:13–14

I recently had a weekend that was spent with a pleasant mix of both old and new friends. I feel like each one of them was brought into my life at a particular time and for a particular reason. God does that for all of us because He knows how much peace a friend can bring. It's as if He leans back in His chair and smiles as He places that perfect puzzle piece into our lives, and it makes what used to be a jumbled mess look like a pretty picture. He's cool like that.

Some friends we may not see for years but can pick right back up where we left off. (They are also the ones who will remember that you used to eat glue.) Some friends we see on a regular basis, like from church, work, or sporting events. We even have "friends" through social media. And then we have the friends that are like family. They are the ones who hold us accountable and keep us in line. God knew how much we would need those friends way before we did.

It is so important to make time for friends. Real time. Sit-by-the-fire-and-talk-until-we-run-out-of-things-to-say time. My girlfriends and I make a point of having a weekend away at least once a year. We've floated on rafts on Lake Cumberland, gone rock climbing in Kentucky, played eighties trivia in a café in Nashville, and sometimes just hung out at whoever's house was kid-free. I used to feel guilty about leaving, but not anymore. Getting a few days to relax and re-boot makes me a better mom and a better wife.

It's also crucial to nurture friendships through a church or a small group. Two of my best friends have done a small group Bible study with me for seventeen years, and they are invaluable. We meet in each other's homes when we can and do three-way phone calls when one of us is out of town. At church, it feels so good to know most everyone's name so I know who to pray for. I love how it's all hands on deck when there is a need in the community, the other side of the country, or the other side of the world. I love how everyone rejoices together when there is a new baptism. There is so much we would miss if we didn't take the time to attend a weekly service and develop and nurture friendships.

Our friends keep us honest and grounded. We have each other's back and build each other up. We call on one another when we need to vent, or cry, or laugh until we cry. We show up in an emergency and drop everything in the middle of the night to help. We counsel with the wisdom that *needs* to be heard instead of just saying what we *want* to hear. We know each other's secrets and love each other anyway. We have probably let each other down but we see beyond the imperfections. We can find the peace and love of Christ through our friends.

Just as Jesus walked this earth with friends, so do we. Thank You, gracious God, for the gift of friendships! Help us have eyes to see those who are lonely and to be a friend to them. Help us always counsel one another with advice that points back to You and brings us peace.

What Is Your Purpose?

The Lord will fulfill his purpose for me; your steadfast love,
O Lord, endures forever. Do not forsake the work of your hands.
PSALM 138:8 ESV

With eight people in our home, the most hectic times in our day are the ones when we're trying to get everyone up and ready to go somewhere. It's funny how everyone has a different morning personality. We have The Snuggler, who always wants to have my arms around them. We have The Instigator, whom we barely notice is awake until they say things like "Someone just took the last of your favorite cereal." We have The Procrastinator, who is in la-la land and needs constant reminders to get ready. We have The Entertainer, who hits the floor running, joke telling, and movie quoting. We have The Conductor, who gives the time every five minutes so nobody is late. We have Indecisive, who drives the Conductor crazy because of countless changes of clothes. We have The Sleepwalker, whom we are not sure is awake for about an hour. I tend to be more Eyes on the Prize. I will trudge through whatever organizing, hair fixing, or homework checking needs to be done to get me to that first cup of coffee. All of these personalities are different and, on the surface, could appear to be annoying. However, each one serves a different purpose.

The Snuggler lets me wake every morning knowing that I'm loved. What a gift! The Instigator notices things that I don't, like when I'm wearing two different shoes. The Procrastinator shows us the beauty

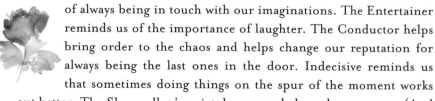

of always being in touch with our imaginations. The Entertainer reminds us of the importance of laughter. The Conductor helps bring order to the chaos and helps change our reputation for always being the last ones in the door. Indecisive reminds us that sometimes doing things on the spur of the moment works out better. The Sleepwalker's quiet demeanor helps calm everyone. (And always brings me coffee.) My focus and organizing helps everyone be able to walk out of the house having homework done, lunches packed, hair fixed, and foreheads kissed. None of us have all of those traits on our own. We need each other. Maybe our purpose for this season of our lives is to balance each other out and help each other grow.

Feeling that our life has purpose gives us a sense of peace. Have you ever wondered what your purpose is? Maybe it's not a grand plan. Maybe it's found in your day-to-day activities. You might think your life is mundane and not making a difference, but maybe you are also doing the humble work. That is profound. You are serving God by serving the people around you. Your life has purpose.

Maybe your purpose today is simply to help someone else find theirs. Maybe today you will smile at a stranger and for the first time this week they won't feel invisible. There are those who are lying in a hospital today. Maybe they are praying their most intimate prayers. Maybe their circumstance drew someone else to pray for the first time. Maybe they are helping their care team to acquire more compassion. What a grand purpose! Even when we don't see the best part of ourselves, others will, and God does. As it says in 2 Thessalonians 3:16, "Now may the Lord of peace himself give you peace at all times and in every way. The Lord be with all of you."

Father God, sometimes I feel like my life has no real purpose. Please let my eyes and heart be opened to how important I am to You and to others. Help me find perfect peace in knowing that You have a plan for my life.

Peace Multiplied

I had a Facebook memory pop up the other day. It said: *Cara is brushing the horses. Joshua's sitting on the porch swing playing with the kittens. Julia and Ben are laughing together in the next room. Emily is wading in the dog's water bucket (again). Surprise visit from my parents, who came with snacks! Paige and Darrin picked me flowers. Beautiful sunset. Everything is doing great in the garden. Happy just watching my world go 'round today!*

You wouldn't guess from reading that post, but there were many storms raging during that time in my life. Day by day, I was learning the hard way to surrender them to God. The definition of surrender is to "cease resistance and submit to authority." That goes against everything our culture tells us, doesn't it? We don't give up! So it took me a long time to realize that surrendering to God's will and laying my battles at the foot of the cross is not being weak. It is finding strength through God's *peace*.

I felt the kind of peace we read about in Psalm 107:29: "He stilled the storm to a whisper; the waves of the sea were hushed." That day, in my little corner of the world, He stilled my storm. God blessed me with perfect peace in everything I had surrendered. I went to bed feeling like my peace was multiplied and not taken away.

Is there anything you need to surrender to God today?

Let us not become weary in doing good,
for at the proper time we will
reap a harvest if we do not give up.

GALATIANS 6:9

Their Walk to Remember

Keep putting into practice all you learned and received from me—
everything you heard from me and saw me doing.
PHILIPPIANS 4:9 NLT

My daughter Julia had childhood apraxia, which made it difficult for her to form sounds and syllables correctly in order to speak. This eventually led to tantrums and crying fits because she would get so frustrated that nobody understood her. She went to speech therapy and a special preschool class, and she learned sign language to try to bridge the communication gap, but still, my little brown-eyed girl often had tear-filled eyes.

During this same time, one of our dear family friends suffered from early onset Alzheimer's. She was at the stage where she understood what you were talking about and could answer yes or no questions but had great difficulty trying to verbally communicate beyond that. One warm summer day I found myself with some free time with just Julia, so we decided to go pick up our friend and go for a walk around the path in our home town.

We started off walking beside the stroller, with Julia swinging her chubby little legs from the seat. Several minutes later, Julia reached up and grabbed our friend's hand, and I immediately saw her face brighten and her expression change. The touch of my child's hand was comfort to her soul. Julia turned and started kicking her legs and motioned to me that she wanted to get down.

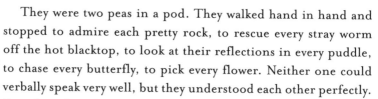

They were two peas in a pod. They walked hand in hand and stopped to admire each pretty rock, to rescue every stray worm off the hot blacktop, to look at their reflections in every puddle, to chase every butterfly, to pick every flower. Neither one could verbally speak very well, but they understood each other perfectly. They followed each other's hand gestures as they pointed to fuzzy caterpillars, chalk drawings, and baby frogs. They watched each other's sparkling eyes to communicate their delight at finding each new treasure. They saw happiness there. Patience. Contentment. Our friend had given my daughter something I couldn't. *Understanding.* She knew exactly what it was like to have great thoughts and ideas and not be able to express them. Each understood the frustration the other was feeling when the rest of the world didn't. Each gave the other permission to take as long as they needed to get the point across. Each laughed in the same language. Pure, innocent, love-filled laughter that I wished I could stash away in a music box and listen to forever.

They were such great teachers! During that walk, I realized that to look into someone's eyes and allow them to have a moment of our time that is just theirs lets them know that they are important and their ideas are valuable. To not be rushed, to recognize God's treasures in the form of funny-shaped clouds and dandelion fluff, to realize the importance of a hug or a pat on the back for a job well done... Those are the things that make life worth living.

I challenge you to not be in a rush today. Slow down long enough to look your loved ones in the eye when they speak. May we notice all of the beauty that we normally take for granted. Pause for a moment to notice how the lights dance off of the rainy streets, or how a bird nested near your window. Take a moment to thank God that it was put there for you to enjoy. Make your next walk one to remember.

Thank You, Lord, for unexpected lessons and unexpected beauty. Help me to always make those around me feel loved, understood, and appreciated. Help me to grow in the virtue of patience.

The Life We Live

*"For I know the plans I have for you," says the Lord.
"They are plans for good and not for disaster,
to give you a future and a hope."*
JEREMIAH 29:11 NLT

Have you ever looked at your life and thought, *How in the world did I
end up here?* Maybe you say it because you are so humbled at how blessed
you are. Or maybe you say it because it isn't *at all* what you planned.
Maybe you are unemployed or have been diagnosed with an illness.
Maybe you didn't think you would be single again. Maybe someone
dear to you has an addiction. Maybe you are grieving. Maybe you have
suffered abuse. I know my life certainly didn't go the way I planned.
I eventually got where I was headed, but God took me the long way
around. Ironically, the long way around meant that I had to go straight
through some really tough times.

I've been a GRIEVING MOM. I had dreamed of being a mother
since the third grade. After I lost my first two babies, the doctor said
I might not be able to have children. I was beyond crushed. But God
was my Comforter and said to be patient in tribulation.

I've been an EXPECTANT MOM. I finally carried to full term.
The pregnancies were exciting, but scary, and I was so sick that I had
to be on IV fluids. I heard God say, "You prayed for this child. Rejoice
in hope." So I did.

I've been a WORKING MOM. For several years I taught special needs children in our public schools, and loved it. I had to step down when I had three children ages three and under, one of whom had special needs. Now I work with my own mom in a completely different field. Who would have thought? But God said that for everything there is a season.

I've been a STAY AT HOME MOM. I got endless snuggles and giggles, but I also got to do things like change endless diapers, break up fights over the red crayon, and fall asleep from exhaustion while standing up in the shower. But God reminded me that the fruit of my labor was the work of His hands.

I've been a HOMESCHOOL MOM. Being both mom and teacher was challenging, but I loved it so. I asked God to show me His patience. Every. Single. Day.

I've been a SINGLE MOM. Never saw that one coming. For a while I worked three part-time jobs and took care of a farm and horses and raised a pitiful garden and the kids on my own. There are no words for how hard that time was, but God gently reminded me that I had a future full of hope.

Eventually I met a wonderful man with a sweet little girl. He asked me to marry him, so now I am a STEPMOM. She is the sweetest girl you could ever meet. God reminded me of His amazing grace.

Sometimes we wonder how our life can look so distorted from the way we pictured it. But *God can see the big picture* that we don't see. Looking back, I realize that I was required to take the long, difficult route sometimes simply because He was improving my character and my faith along the way. I had to learn to be patient in His answer and to trust in His plan. No matter how distorted the picture of your life may seem to you now, know that God is not finished with you yet.

Dear God, I know that Your plans for me are bigger than my own, but sometimes it is so hard to wait on Your answer. Help me to patiently trust in You.

Going Old School

Do you see someone who speaks in haste?
There is more hope for a fool than for them.
PROVERBS 29:20

When my family moved into an old farmhouse, there was a rotary dial phone hanging on the wall. I have a picture of the kids standing around it, trying to figure it out. I showed them how to twirl your finger all the way around the dial before you found the next number. They could not believe that it took soooo long to dial. They kept saying things like "You mean you sat next to the wall? For the entire conversation?" Yep. "You couldn't see the person on the other end of the line?" Nope. "You couldn't text them?" Nope.

When I was a kid, if I didn't know the answer to a question, I had to talk to an adult or go to the library and research it. This generation just asks Siri. When we click on a link on the Internet, if it takes longer than three to six seconds, we move on to another link. With short attention spans and instant answers, it's hard to learn the value of patience. We often find ourselves in sticky situations because we tend to make quick decisions too.

These days we can get fast food twenty-four hours a day, but there is something to be said for weeding and watering a garden all season, waiting for just the right time to harvest. A text reaches someone in seconds, but sometimes it's better to hear the sound of the other person's voice on the phone. We can post pictures on Instagram, but isn't it nice to have framed photographs to hand down through the generations? We can upload a book on our Kindle, but there's something about holding one in your hands and feeling and smelling it that makes you not want to put it down.

Times sure are changing, but there are some things that are only learned by doing things the old-fashioned way. Chivalry. Manners. Humility. Patience. Empathy. Those are things that we don't learn from Siri. There are certain things that we learn only from our family and from God. We learn from sitting at the kitchen table and listening to Grandma tell stories about her childhood. Or teaching a little one to tie their shoes. Or sticking up for a younger brother. Or helping a sister mend a broken heart. We learn by taking care of a sick parent. Or giving someone a sincere apology. Or doing extra chores. Or burying our favorite pet.

Sometimes technology is great, and sometimes we just need to put it down and learn things old school. This week, talk with someone in person. Share a conversation over an actual cup of coffee instead of sending them an emoji of one. If you are about to make an important decision, pray about it for a while and make sure emotion isn't getting in the way. Philippians 4:6 tells us, "Do not be anxious about anything, but in every situation, by prayer and petition, with thanksgiving, present your requests to God." My grandmother always told me that anything too small to be made in to a prayer is too small to be made into a burden. No prayer is too small! Then run it by a trusted friend with Godly counsel and ask for their opinion. If it still sounds like a good idea, then it probably is the right thing to do.

Dear heavenly Father, sometimes it's difficult to discern whether my actions are what You want me to do or whether I'm finding ways to justify them because they're what I want to do. Help me to always seek You first, and to be patient in awaiting Your answer.

Give Me Patience

Eggs go in your mouth, not your nose.

Snakes stay outside.

We do not wash our hands in the dog bowl.

Let's carry the frog in a bucket, not your pants.

You would think those are sentences that wouldn't have to be said out loud, but it's one of those parts of raising children that nobody prepares you for. Ephesians 4:2 tells us to "be completely humble and gentle; be patient, bearing with one another in love." That sure is easier said than done! God did not just *give* me patience. I struggle with it every day. He has, however, given me many opportunities to *practice* patience. There are sentences God probably didn't think He would have to say to me either!

Make time for Me before other things.

Pray for guidance before you react.

You are not God. Quit acting like it.

That whisper is the Holy Spirit. Listen.

I'm thankful for His unending patience, and hope to do better in following His lead. So when my child asks me to sing "Coat of Many Colors" to her six times tonight, I will do it. Again. And when my dad tells everyone that he had to tie a pork chop around my neck to get the dog to play with me, I'll laugh. Again. (I do love his jokes.) I'll try to remember the many times that *they* have had to be patient with *me*.

What can you do to practice patience today?

kindness

All of you, be like-minded,

be sympathetic,

love one another,

be compassionate and humble.

1 Peter 3:8

Three Things

Therefore, as God's chosen people, holy and dearly loved,
clothe yourselves with compassion,
kindness, humility, gentleness and patience.
COLOSSIANS 3:12

One day I was at a red light in town and my twelve-year-old son, Ben, was with me. We noticed a woman walk up to a storefront pushing a wheelchair and having trouble getting through the door. Ben said, "She's not going to be able to get that door open. I'm helping her. Come back around for me." Without hesitation, he jumped out of the car and held the door so she could maneuver the wheelchair into the store. It brought tears to my eyes. In that moment, I got a glimpse of the man my boy would grow up to be. He wasn't thinking about who was watching, or if he knew this person, or if he would make it back to the car before the light turned green. He was being God's light. It is one of the most important things that I've tried to instill in my children since they were small, and it made my heart smile to see him do it so effortlessly.

Making a conscious decision to "be a light" started several years ago, when I would ask my kids to tell me three good things about their day before they went to bed. They might have noticed a pretty sunset, the smell of the fresh air, or the softness of their favorite blanket. They could always come up with three.

Over the years, that conversation evolved from telling three good things that happened *to* them, to telling three good things they did *around* them that day. Three acts of kindness. Three ways they were God's light to others. We go around the dinner table and I ask everyone to share what they did. Sometimes if I forget, at least one of them will say, "Aren't you going to ask me what my three things are today?" It's so fun to see how their acts of kindness have grown. Being kind is becoming part of their character. When I see them showing true compassion and kindness to others when they don't think I'm looking, it lets me know that as a parent, I got this part right.

The other day I walked in to tell my son Joshua good night and found him writing in a journal that I didn't know he had. Every single sentence on every single page for every single day started with "Today I am happy because..." Except one. The last sentence said, "God answered my prayers." My mama heart burst at the seams! He gets it.

At work one day we got an email from our CEO, who suggested that all employees keep a personal journal to document the good things that happened to them each day. He said to write things down before we start our day and then read over them and add to them before we go to bed. What a great idea! A journal full of blessings that we may have forgotten otherwise. Often we can be told a hundred compliments and one negative comment, and the negative is the one we remember. Writing down the positives can help keep things in perspective when we find ourselves feeling vulnerable or defeated. What are your three things?

Thank You, Jesus, for showing us what perfect kindness looks like. It's easy to be nice to people who are nice to us, but You showed us how to love everyone. Help me to always find ways to extend Your kindness to others.

Be the One

For everyone who exalts himself will be humbled,
but the one who humbles himself will be exalted.
LUKE 14:11

Last year I had to have a bone replaced in my neck. I had heard great stories about things my surgeon had done for former patients, and soon enough I got to see firsthand how true they were. Since he specialized in neck and back injuries, he had his patients walk barefoot so he could pinpoint the problem by studying their gait. He insisted on both removing and replacing their socks and shoes so they didn't have to lean over to do it themselves. There is something very humbling about helping someone with their stinky feet. Every time he did this for me, it reminded me of when Jesus washed the feet of His disciples.

The day of my follow-up appointment, I was so sick that I had my husband call to cancel. It was the last scheduled visit for the day, and the surgeon insisted I make the hour-long drive to come in anyway. I was so mad! I had a fever, had lost nearly twenty pounds, and could barely pick myself up off the bathroom floor. Was he just trying to be sure he got paid that day? But my husband drove me in anyway. During the appointment, I voiced my frustration. He said that if I hadn't come in, he would have sent me to the ER to make sure I wasn't sick from infection due to the surgery. The wait at the hospital would have been several hours and the chance of leaving with an infection

would have been greater. He didn't want me to go through that.

How incredibly selfish I felt! This high-demand, world-renowned surgeon not only saved me from going to the ER but stayed after hours to help me. I cried as I overheard him telling his staff that he would pay for their dinner if they could stay late. Then he stood by me and told me stories about his family while we waited for my husband to drive to the local drugstore. He wanted to make sure I had nausea medicine for the ride home. It was well after dark when I was finally well enough to get back in the car. I felt awful for being mad at him earlier. I should have known better. His prestige did not keep him from being humble.

One of the definitions of humble is "showing that you do not think of yourself as better than other people." Let us not forget to do the humble things in life. If the day comes that we think we are too good to show kindness to the people around us, I hope someone very lovingly knocks us right off that pedestal.

Be the one who changes that empty roll of toilet paper and scrubs that stain out of the toilet. Be the one who smiles at the homeless man you pass every morning and brings him a cup of hot chocolate on a cold day. Be the one who reaches out to the single mom who desperately needs help with a project around the house. Be the one to send a Valentine to the widow who will not have one for the first time. Be the one who shovels the driveway for an elderly neighbor without their having to ask. Be the one to write a thank-you note to your doctor. Be the one.

God, I am thankful that You surround me with people who show me kindness even when I am feeling unkind. You said that whatever we do for the least of Your people, we do for You. Help me be the one who helps those most in need.

Practice Kindness

Be kind and compassionate to one another,
forgiving each other, just as in Christ God forgave you.
EPHESIANS 4:32

The check-out line of a store is where you often see a person's true character. One day the lady running the register in my line was working incredibly slowly. The man in front of me was grumbling, and when it was his turn, he slammed his items down. He was loud and made sure everyone around him knew what a bad job he thought she was doing. He cursed everyone as he walked out.

When it was my turn, she apologized for being slow. She said she was waiting on a transplant operation and was in terrible pain. She was really too sick to be there but couldn't afford not to work because if she was lucky enough to get the organ she needed, she would have to be off work for a long time. She didn't have anyone to take care of her, so she was going to have to pay for assisted living. She was afraid she'd lose her home.

You never know what heartache a person is going through. Be kind. That woman couldn't control her health or the fact that she didn't have family to help. She couldn't control this man's rudeness towards her. But she could control her attitude about it. Instead of lashing out, she chose to be grateful for her job. She chose to use kind words towards him and remain professional. She was already thankful for the operation she had yet to receive. She was preparing her heart and her mind for the good and chose not to make room for the negative. She was the perfect example of the fact that a positive attitude and the fruit of the Spirit is something that has to be practiced.

Another day, I was walking alone, enjoying quiet reflection time with God. I tend to get emotional during those walks, because that's when my deepest joys and deepest sorrows come to the surface to be lifted up to Him. When I rounded the corner of the trail, I noticed a lovely lady, bent over and pulling leaves out of a drainage ditch. I recognized that she lived in the senior home near the path. I said, "I bet you had lots of land where you lived before." She replied, "Yes! How did you know?" I told her that she seemed like an outdoor kind of gal because she was working in a ditch with no gloves. That led to a conversation about my grandmother, and she could see my eyes tear up. She said, "You miss her, don't you?" I could barely whisper, "Very much," through the lump in my throat. Then she said, "I've seen you sitting on your back porch before, and you looked like you were crying. I prayed for you." Then she hugged me, and the floodgates opened. Our family had gone through a very difficult year, and this stranger had noticed and prayed for me. And at that moment, embracing this woman whose name I didn't know, I felt every one of those prayers. She had no idea how much her kindness meant to me.

Friends, it takes just as much time to say something kind as it does to say something hurtful. Find time today to show kindness to a person you don't know, to your family, and to yourself. Do a random act of kindness and don't tell anyone about it. God knows.

Dear Lord, sometimes our emotions get the best of us and we take our anger out on those who don't deserve it. Help me to remember that everyone is going through something, and to be kind in all circumstances.

Being God's Hands

A couple of years ago, I had surgery that required me to be off my feet. When there are six children to take care of and Mom is out of commission, it puts a lot of extra work on Dad. To our surprise, a friend made some arrangements and meals began to show up at our home every night. Some were from people we knew, and some were from people we had just met at our new church. Feeding a family of eight is no small task, so it was such a blessing to get that help! Matthew 25:35—36 says, "For I was hungry and you gave me something to eat, I was thirsty and you gave me something to drink, I was a stranger and you invited me in, I needed clothes and you clothed me, I was sick and you looked after me, I was in prison and you came to visit me." Those who fed us were being God's hands and showing God's kindness, asking nothing in return.

It's wonderful when kindness is shown to us, but it's even better when we can demonstrate it to others. Just after my youngest had turned three, we were working on an "acts of kindness" project around town. She woke one morning, walked into the kitchen, stretched, and said, "So what are we gonna do to make other people happy today?" Be still, my heart!

How can you be God's hands of kindness today?

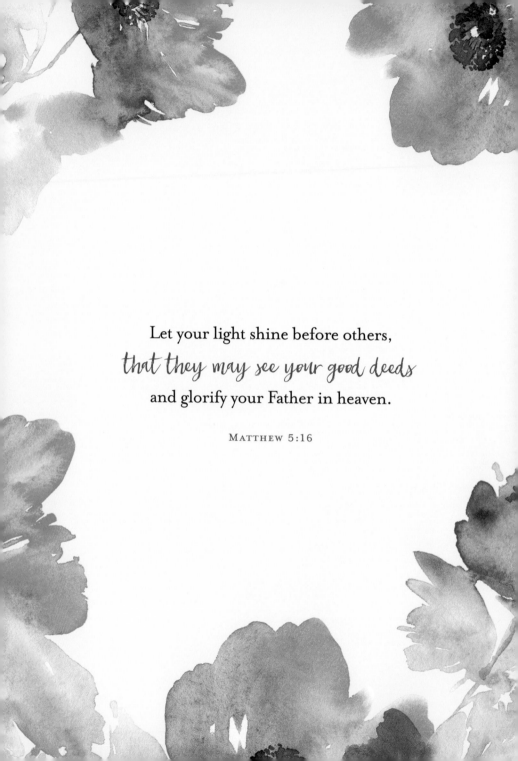

Let your light shine before others,
that they may see your good deeds
and glorify your Father in heaven.

MATTHEW 5:16

The Power of Invisibility

Every good and perfect gift is from above,
coming down from the Father of the heavenly lights,
who does not change like shifting shadows.
JAMES 1:17

Since my son was old enough to understand what a superhero was, he wanted to be Spiderman. He figured someone had to fill that Spidey suit, so it might as well be him. So when he was six, he found a mysterious package addressed to him. In it was a cape and mask, along with a letter that said if he really believed in the power to do good things for other people, he could also be a superhero. See, the cape gave him the superpower of invisibility.

For weeks, our little man would put on his cape and zip around doing good deeds around the house, knowing that nobody could see that it was him doing it. He got no credit because none of us actually saw him in action. But he got to stand next to us as we found the results of his good deeds and see how happy it made us, and that was his reward.

I have wished many times over the years that I could have the power of invisibility. Like when my kids were jumping around behind people at the ball game yelling the diarrhea song. Or when my five-year-old walked into church and swatted the pastor's backside to say hello, in true locker-room fashion. I used to picture raising a sweet, quiet family, but that's just not who we are. We are the ones who have wet toilet paper fights out the bedroom windows. Our kids have been known to eat bugs and cat food. On purpose. We love practical jokes and wedgies and singing at the top of our lungs. Yep. We are that family. And I wouldn't trade it for the world.

So I'm rethinking my wish to have the power of invisibility. It's true that I got the stink eye when one of my kids tackled the other in the library, but I also got to stand right beside them, clearly visible, when they spent hours clipping coupons to make sure the money they were donating to the pregnancy center bought as many supplies as possible. Somewhere a single mom who chose to keep her baby got new clothes and diapers. Or when they boxed care packages to send to our military serving overseas, and somewhere a soldier got a taste of home when they opened a surprise package filled with handwritten notes, magazines, toiletries, games, and food items. Or when they raised money to purchase trees to replace the ones lost by neighbors, and spent an entire day planting in the cold and rain. Or when they dropped off new items to the homeless shelter, or spent the day doing random acts of kindness around town, or donated items to the local animal shelter.

One day, the trees they planted will stand tall, just as I can now, when I say, "Yep. Those kids over there having a spitting contest are mine." They chose goodness and didn't really tell anyone about it. They did it with their invisibility capes on. So I ask you, what is your superpower? What good deeds can you do under the cape of invisibility today?

Dear heavenly Father, You may seem to be invisible to us when we don't give it much thought, but when we pay attention, we can see all good things come from You. When the beauty of nature holds us in awe, when one person reaches out to serve another, when new life is brought into the world, when the broken are made whole, that is when You are incredibly visible. Thank You for Your goodness.

Finding the Significance

O Lord, what a variety of things you have made!
In wisdom you have made them all.
The earth is full of your creatures.
PSALM 104:24 NLT

I was cleaning out the car the other day and found a handful of rocks in my cup holder. And another one in the cup holder in the back. And another one in the side door. I noticed more sitting on the work bench in the garage. My daughter saw me starting to throw them out and said, "Stop! You can't throw that away! That's the one I picked up the day you and me picked flowers on our breakfast walk." Ahh, I remembered then. We were in Wisconsin and had gotten up before everyone else. I grabbed my coffee and she grabbed a bucket, and we walked through the woods and picked flowers and caught frogs. The bucket was full of both by the time we got back. The same day I was cleaning out my car here in Ohio, my mom called from the Wisconsin house where we had been a few weeks earlier. She said she found rocks hidden all over the place. I guess this was just something my kids did that I hadn't really noticed before.

So I started paying attention and realized that rocks are all over our home. On top of the picture frame hanging in the foyer. In a bowl on the counter. In the pockets of jeans in the laundry. On top of dressers and in bags on closet floors. I asked the kids about them and realized they aren't crazy rock collectors. They've been collecting memories.

My youngest isn't old enough to keep a journal, but she can tell you a story about each and every one of those rocks she picked up, and the other kids can tell you about theirs too. They know where we were when we found them, and what we were doing when they picked them up. It means that they were noticing the importance of a special moment while it was happening, and it brought tears to my eyes. The value of those otherwise insignificant gray and brown rocks skyrocketed when they tied them to a memory. Memories gave the rocks significance and made them beautiful.

It got me wondering if I do a good job letting my family know that our time together is valuable to me. Do they know their significance in my life? How often do I say things like:

I cherish our time together.
You are so much fun!
I enjoy our talks.
You make me happy.
You're a great person.
I believe in you.
I love you.

God's goodness is all around us! We must take time to notice its significance. We will never regret taking more time with our loved ones, but we might regret the time we wasted looking at our phones or sleeping the day away or passing up invitations to join in. My kids could have easily passed by that old gray rock, and it would have lain there for many years. But they saw its significance and its beauty. They saw that it was good. They picked it up, made a memory out of it, and gave it meaning. How can we do the same for those we care about?

Dear Lord, thank You for picking me up when I feel insignificant and making me beautiful. Help me to recognize the importance of a special moment while it's happening. Help me to hold onto it, memorize it, retell it, and note its significance in my life. Help me to make it a part of my story.

I Believe in You

Finally, brothers and sisters, whatever is true, whatever is noble,
whatever is right, whatever is pure, whatever is lovely, whatever is admirable—
if anything is excellent or praiseworthy—think about such things.

PHILIPPIANS 4:8

At a recent visit to an amusement park, it didn't take long for me to see how different people really are. Some outward differences were apparent, such as their haircuts, tattoos, and fashion. However, after standing next to the same people for an hour or more, you start to see their inward differences too, such as their sense of humor and level of patience (or lack thereof). Some people were kind, even to strangers. Instead of just seeing another face in the crowd, they seemed to really see the person behind it. One lady even let me use her coupon while ordering pizzas for eight teenagers, because my bill was pretty lofty. Then others were very "every-man-for-himself" and would push and shove their way to the front, causing even the patient people to get annoyed. It was ironic to me that even with all of those differences, we were all standing in line for the big coasters, so we had at least that one thing in common. Maybe we all have more in common than we think. Deep down, don't we all want the same things? To be heard. To be loved. To feel important. To be respected. To have at least one person we know we can trust and count on no matter what. To know that our life matters. To know that someone believes in us.

When I was a special needs teacher, I had one rule for every student

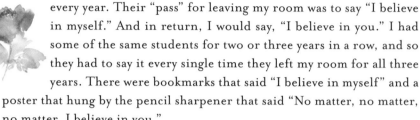

every year. Their "pass" for leaving my room was to say "I believe in myself." And in return, I would say, "I believe in you." I had some of the same students for two or three years in a row, and so they had to say it every single time they left my room for all three years. There were bookmarks that said "I believe in myself" and a poster that hung by the pencil sharpener that said "No matter, no matter, no matter, I believe in you."

I had no way of knowing at the time if those words would ever sink in, but the mother of one of my former students came up to me at a volleyball game just last year. She told me that her son is now in college and making really good grades, and that she credits a large part of his school success to those years with me because I helped him believe in himself and gain confidence. She is a really great mom, so I know that's not all on me, but what an absolute honor! The thing is, we never really know how much we will change someone else's life with just a few encouraging words.

I still remember the leader of my Brownie troop telling us that we should not leave a room the way we found it. We should leave it better. Shouldn't it be the same way with the people we come in contact with? Whether it be a stranger standing in line next to us, or the people we share a home with, or those we work with every day, we have an opportunity to build them up. There are a lot of things in life that we will probably never be able to afford, but kindness, courtesy, love, and respect don't cost us a thing. What can you do today to help someone else stand a little taller?

Dear God, thank You for believing in me those times I don't even believe in myself. Help me to always model Your perfect goodness to others.

Licked Clean

One day my three-year-old walked in with a big red strawberry. She said, "Here, Mommy! I picked this just for you." With sparkling eyes, she watched me eat it. When I hugged her and told her how good it was, she said, "I knew you would like it because I licked it all clean for you." (She's lucky she's so adorable.)

Goodness can look many different ways. We can see the goodness of God's creation all around us, like when His artwork is displayed across the sky before He puts the sun to bed. We recognize the goodness in someone's heart, like when my son taped eleven pennies into my birthday card. It was all he had to give. We can taste goodness in our favorite home-cooked meal. (Or even in a freshly "cleaned" strawberry.)

Psalm 100:5 reminds us that the Lord is *always* good. Since we are made in His image, His goodness is a part of us. We are to show goodness to others, even when they aren't good to us. Romans 12:20–21 says, "If your enemy is hungry, feed him; if he is thirsty, give him something to drink. In doing this, you will heap burning coals on his head. Do not be overcome by evil, but overcome evil with good."

Let us exude goodness until others cannot help but see God in us. What goodness do you see around you today? How can you show goodness to others?

faithfulness

What does the LORD your God ask of you
but to fear the LORD your God,
to walk in obedience to him, to love him,
to serve the LORD your God
with all your heart and with all your soul,
and to observe the LORD's commands and decrees
that I am giving you today for your own good?

DEUTERONOMY 10:12–13

Enjoy the Storm

When Jesus spoke again to the people, he said,
"I am the light of the world. Whoever follows me
will never walk in darkness, but will have the light of life."
JOHN 8:12

My Grandma Forrest lived in the deepest part of the north woods of Wisconsin, where our family has spent many days sitting on the front porch swing singing songs like "How Great Thou Art" and "Amazing Grace." Every once in a while, a big "northern" storm would blow in and we would all run into the house. But not Grandma. That's when she would go into the kitchen and make popcorn and tell us to meet her out on the porch. At first I wasn't so sure about volunteering for that, but she said, "Even storms can be beautiful," and before I knew it, we were all out on the front porch with the lights out and popcorn in our laps. Within minutes, we saw what she was talking about.

When lightning flashes through complete and total darkness like that, you are able to see way back through the trees in a way that you are unable to in the daylight. The dark that looked like a sea of scary nothingness turns into an amazing light display where you are instantly aware of your beautiful surroundings and no longer afraid of what you can't see. For me, it only took one time of joining her on the porch to learn to enjoy the storm like she did.

Over the years, my grandma witnessed many "storms" in her life, but she had a way of finding the beauty in the midst of life's storms

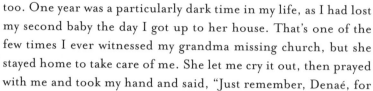

too. One year was a particularly dark time in my life, as I had lost my second baby the day I got up to her house. That's one of the few times I ever witnessed my grandma missing church, but she stayed home to take care of me. She let me cry it out, then prayed with me and took my hand and said, "Just remember, Denaé, for every Good Friday of your life, there will always be an Easter Sunday." Her faith was always strong, and she knew that just like the "northerns" that blew streaks of light through the woods, the light of Christ would make even the worst kind of darkness more clear and less scary.

When we got the news that my grandmother was sick, it was our turn to hold her hand and pray. I was crying my eyes out, because I couldn't imagine life without her. I was being selfish. I wanted her here! It felt like I was a kid again, sitting in the scary nothingness of the dark, afraid of what I couldn't see. But she wasn't crying. She knew that dark news was no match for God's light. She wasn't afraid because her faith made her aware of the beauty in the midst of the storm that we call the dying process.

I still sit out on that front porch in Wisconsin every chance I get. Now I sit there with my own family and try to never forget the popcorn. Storms will always come. That's just part of life. Sometimes it seems hopeless. Sometimes it's scary. Sometimes we are so very afraid of what we can't see. But today I challenge you to keep looking through the darkness. Even storms can be beautiful. Look for the Light. He always comes.

Dear gracious God, thank You for being the Light that renews my spirit and my faith. Help me to always feel Your presence in the storms of my life, and to praise You through it all.

Would You Rather?

The LORD himself goes before you and will be with you;
he will never leave you nor forsake you.
Do not be afraid; do not be discouraged.
DEUTERONOMY 31:8

A couple of years ago our family got the game called Would You Rather. It's a game of questions where players are given a choice and have to answer which one they would rather do. The questions run something like this: "Would you rather eat a moldy pancake or chew an old piece of bubble gum off the sidewalk?" or "Would you rather find true love or a winning lottery ticket?" It's a fun family game that helps you get to know each other better.

Long after the game is put away, I find myself creating my own Would You Rather questions in my head. Would I rather have a huge house that's always clean, or my average house with little fingerprints on the walls? Would I rather have endless patience or endless time? Would I rather have my kids see me as a perfect parent or see me as a flawed human being? Would I rather be able to solve all of my children's problems or let them learn their own lessons? Most of the answers were easy, but the last couple were not.

Would I rather have my kids see me as a perfect parent? I used to think so, but not anymore. It's okay for them to see me mess up sometimes, as long as I can also show them how to make better choices to make it right again. I share stories with them about lessons

I learned the hard way, and let them see my fallibility. That way, they know it's okay when they aren't perfect too. I want them to see me apologize and watch how I handle things when I feel like I'm not measuring up to the world's standards. Because, guess what? A lot of times the world's standards aren't good standards to begin with.

Would I rather solve all of my kids' problems? For most of their younger years, I did just that. I was always playing offense to shield them from harm before it could even *think* of coming their way, and when it did, I was on the first line of defense. But I want them to look to God as their first line of defense, not me. I want them to see that He is *always* leading them, even when I can't.

Sometimes when I think about my past I think I would have rather made a different choice about certain things. Maybe the outcome would have been better. Maybe not. One thing's for sure: The heartache helped me learn compassion. Sickness helped me appreciate being well, and to reach out to those who are not. Traumatizing parts let me realize the strength of my faith. Having to rely on others let me learn humility and to grow a heart that would reach out to others in need. Being at rock bottom let me lean completely on God.

So what would I rather do? I'd rather teach my family to put their faith in God instead of always in me. I'm only human. I don't always have the right answers, or make the right choices, or say the right things, but God always does. What would you rather do?

Dear God, thank You for showing me that I do not face trials alone. You are my Father, my doctor, my counselor, my friend, and my defense attorney. Help me to seek Your counsel for wisdom and discernment to make the right choices.

Been There, Done That

If you are faithful in little things, you will be faithful in large ones.
LUKE 16:10 NLT

One beautiful fall day, a group of us went hiking and rock climbing in the hills of Kentucky. As my friend and I stood at the bottom of the rock taking pictures of the teenagers making the climb ahead of us, she was telling me that she didn't think she could make it. However, her son was having none of that. He knew she was scared, but he also knew that her fear was a bigger obstacle than the rock. When she told him that she wasn't going to go, he said, "Mom, you can do this. I'll help you." He believed in her until she believed in herself. As I watched them from the bottom of the rock, I could hear him cheering his mom on.

You've got this!

Keep going.

You're going to be okay.

You're doing great!

Don't quit, you're almost there.

She had faith in him, and he guided her up the rock, showing her where to place each foot and what to grab onto in order to make the climb safely and steadily. She did it afraid. What an awesome feeling when they got to the top and conquered that fear together! I believe that fear and courage go hand in hand. If my friend had never been fearful about climbing that rock, then she wouldn't have had to dig up the courage to climb it. Fear ignites courage. Courage helps us overcome our fears. So the trick to confronting a fear head on is to find the source of your courage. Where does your courage come from?

I believe it can come from experience, from our encouragers, and above all else, from God. I've found that I have to be intentional in how I handle my fear. When I try to tackle it on my own, I can build up so much anxiety that I physically pass out. However, when I seek God's help first, He lets me see that even if my fear is bigger than me, it's not bigger than Him. Just as my friend's son helped her climb the rock, if we put our trust in God, He guides us, showing us where to place each foot and what to grab onto in order to overcome our challenges safely and steadily. Instead of being a rock that is an obstacle in front of us, He is our Rock in whom we can always trust. "Have I not commanded you? Be strong and courageous. Do not be afraid; do not be discouraged, for the LORD your God will be with you wherever you go" (Joshua 1:9).

That doesn't mean it's not going to be scary. It simply means we know we are not going through it alone, and we can square up, even if we have to do it afraid. The good thing is that once we have gotten through something that is really scary, it's not so scary anymore. I bet my friend would climb that rock again. Once we put our faith and trust in God, we know what we are capable of with His strength. We have wisdom in how to handle it if it should happen again. We become the encourager for others who will go through the same thing. We were there. We conquered it. We overcame. We had faith. It feels good.

My God, my Rock, my Fortress, thank You for giving me courage when I have none. Thank You for being my strength when I am weak. Help me to face my fears with the faith of Your guidance.

A Favorable Time

If I was being completely honest, I'd have to say that faithfulness to God has been a struggle at certain times in my life. Second Timothy 4:2 tells us to "Preach the word of God. Be prepared, whether the time is favorable or not" (NLT). Sometimes when it was inconvenient I just didn't do it. I didn't want to offend someone, or wanted to fit in, or wanted to justify an action by human reasoning instead of God's truth. That never ends well.

Sometimes I feel so close to God that tears well up because I'm so humbled by His love. Other times I feel so distant that I don't even want to read His Word. But here's the thing. God never changes. He's always there, just where He's always been. The Holy Spirit is in my heart whether I always recognize it or not. If there is a feeling of distance, it was created by me. The good thing is, He's always there with open arms when I'm ready to come back.

I'm thankful that my parents never allowed the question in our house to be *"Are* we going to church?" It was only *"What time* are we going to church?" It made our faith a priority and gave me roots that sustained me in hard times. I've learned to thank God *ahead of time* for the prayers He will answer. "As for me and my household, we will serve the Lord" (Joshua 24:15).

Thank God *ahead of time* for something today.

gentleness

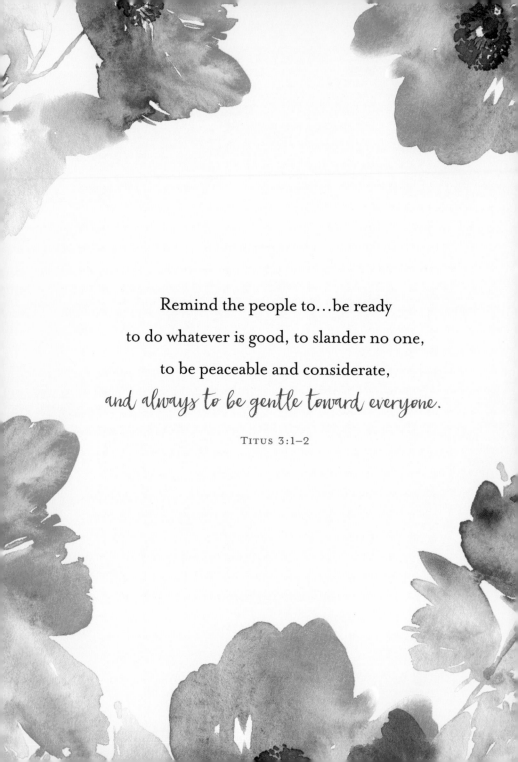

Remind the people to…be ready
to do whatever is good, to slander no one,
to be peaceable and considerate,
and always to be gentle toward everyone.

Titus 3:1–2

I Will Remember This Snuggle

Whoever welcomes this little child in my name welcomes me;
and whoever welcomes me welcomes the one who sent me.
For it is the one who is least among you all who is the greatest.
LUKE 9:48

It was a moment that may not have unfolded in the morning routine of most days.

Getting six kids ready for school and myself ready for work normally looks like three hours of nonstop rushing. It's generally full of alarms, missing socks, someone banging on the bathroom door, brushing teeth, fixing hair, finding lost homework, remembering to grab the lunchboxes, writing that note I forgot the night before, finding the razor someone (nobody) took without permission, looking for the other shoe, and trying not to miss the bus. But in my recent efforts to make *sure* my kids know the value of faith, family, and friends over schedules, iPhones, and YouTube, *this day* I stopped what I was doing and listened when my five-year-old walked into my bathroom when I was fixing my hair for work and asked if I'd sit down and hold her. My usual response might have been "Not right now... I have to finish getting ready so I'm not late." But not today. This time I looked down at my baby girl looking up at me and saw how fast she was growing. I decided that my hair was good enough for today and my response was "Of course I will."

So we pulled out the chair that she normally uses to kneel on when

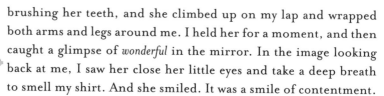

brushing her teeth, and she climbed up on my lap and wrapped both arms and legs around me. I held her for a moment, and then caught a glimpse of *wonderful* in the mirror. In the image looking back at me, I saw her close her little eyes and take a deep breath to smell my shirt. And she smiled. It was a smile of contentment. Her sleepy little voice said, "Mama…when I miss you today, I'm going to think about how you smell and remember this snuggle." So will I, baby girl. So will I.

In that moment that almost didn't happen, I realized that what other people might think is cheap, vanilla, drug store perfume represents comfort, security, and love to my daughter. I realized that taking a few extra minutes out of my usual morning routine didn't make a bit of difference to the rest of the world, but it meant the world to her. I went to work with my hair in a ponytail and wearing a bracelet made out of a hairband and barrettes, but with the satisfaction? joy? of knowing that my child knew she was the most important thing in that moment. It took only a few minutes to make a memory.

Friends, today I encourage you to make a point to slow down. In the rush of your daily routine, take time to give hugs and kisses good-bye. It only take a few seconds to do but could change the whole course of someone's day. Maybe that someone is you. I encourage you to pray together before a meal. Sit at the table and not in front of the television. You never know what might unfold when a few moments of "rush" are taken out of your day.

Dear heavenly Father, thank You for gentle reminders of how precious small moments can be. Help me to not be rushed, so that I don't miss the blessings You have placed all around me. During the times when I am stressed out and overwhelmed, help me to remember that I am Your child, and You are my Father. Help me to feel Your loving arms around me, as if I'm snuggled on Your lap.

The Power of Forgiveness

For if you forgive other people when they sin against you,
your heavenly Father will also forgive you.
MATTHEW 6:14

Giving true forgiveness is so hard. It's something I have to continue to work on, and hope to get better at every day. Human nature tells us to hold a grudge or get even, so forgiveness does not come easily, and it doesn't happen automatically. It's a choice. Sometimes we feel like whoever wronged us does not deserve to be forgiven. They don't get a free pass for what they did. We let bitterness set up camp in our minds and harden our hearts. And to what end? It holds us hostage. And in most cases, the person who wronged us is going along with their lives without a care for what they did, so this holding back forgiveness business is usually not punishing anyone but ourselves.

It took me a long time to realize that forgiving someone does not mean that what they did is okay. It's not saying that we no longer care what happened or that we want to associate with that person again. Forgiveness doesn't free them from the consequences. That's between them and God. What it does is free us from the anger. It helps us heal. It allows us to choose peace and move on. It is not a sign of weakness. It takes a strong person to be gentle enough to forgive.

I've never really liked the expression "Forgive and forget." If we've truly forgiven, we should not keep bringing it up, but I don't think we should necessarily forget it either. Remembering what we did wrong, the humility of it, how we may have hurt someone, and then remembering how we made it right again is how we grow. It's how we remember not to do it again. It's how we forgive ourselves. It's how we teach our children to not make the same mistakes.

Consider this. When have we been forgiven by others when *we* didn't deserve it? God does it for us all the time. That is the gift of grace. And when have we *not* been given a punishment when we *did* deserve it? God does that for us all the time too. That is the gift of mercy. We learn the power of forgiveness through the grace and mercy God shows to us, so that we can do the same for others.

What if the other person isn't sorry? What if they never gave you a well-deserved apology? Forgive them anyway. What if they keep giving you new reasons to loathe them? Then you can choose to forgive them again. It isn't really for them. It's for you. It gives you permission to move on without carrying the burden of someone else's actions.

Sometimes others do the same for me and sometimes they don't. I can't control their actions, but I can control mine. When I think forgiveness is never going to happen, I try to choose it again. And again. I choose it until it finally takes, and it usually does. Sometimes it takes a great leap of faith, and sometimes it just takes me getting over my own ego. Sometimes I even find myself praying for them, and that's when I know the true healing process has begun. Grace and mercy. I pray that I can both give and receive them when needed.

Is there anyone you need to be gentle enough to forgive? Do you need to ask for anyone's forgiveness?

Dear gracious God, thank You for forgiving me, even when I don't deserve it. Help me to always recognize how Your grace and mercy are working in my own life so that I can extend grace and mercy to others.

A Matter of Perspective

*Fathers, do not provoke your children to anger
by the way you treat them. Rather, bring them up
with the discipline and instruction that comes from the Lord.*

Ephesians 6:4 nlt

I stumbled upon a post today from December of 2012, and the reminder came to me at exactly the time I needed it. It said: *Ben got up before I did and hung up all the stockings for me, but only after he drew all over them with a Sharpie. I was mad, but someone told me, "When you're old and gray you'll look back on those stockings and remember your little boy." So true. Such a good reminder to not sweat the small stuff. If anything, it just made a memory. Today, I'm just going to enjoy them being little.*

Maybe I need to let the wise words of my friend sink in. Did it really matter if the stockings had marker on them? No. He was just trying to write our names to surprise me that morning the only way he knew how. In my tendency to always want things done a certain way, I missed his sweet gesture. If I had changed my perspective, it would have changed the whole outcome. In fact, I can change my perspective on a lot of things. Instead of focusing on how something got broken, I need to look at the little person behind it, who is just human and didn't mean to. Instead of getting angry about how much time we have to spend doing homework when I'd rather be outside, I need to remember that one day, nobody will need my help with homework anymore.

Raising a family and balancing schedules is hard work, but it is a privilege, not an obligation. Yes, it's aggravating when you feel taken for granted, or when you've reminded them a dozen times to do something and they still forget. It's hard to sit and watch them do something the wrong way, but they have to learn. How many times do we expect God to do the very same thing for us? In many ways, we are still those stubborn children who mess up over and over before we learn, who insist on doing things the wrong way, who forget to say we're sorry and take our Father for granted. Practicing grace and mercy, patience and humility, gently seeing our own flaws reflected back from another person, and admitting to our mistakes sure does have a way of softening a heart.

When I look through old pictures of my kids when they were much smaller, I think how much I'd like to have those moments back. And then I realize that one day in the future I will be looking through a photo album and want *these* moments back. These. Right now. The ones where our family is all here to make s'mores around the campfire and ride four-wheelers in the woods. The ones where my teenage kids always come up to hug me good night and talk with me about their day. The ones where the little ones still ask for me to tuck them in and say bedtime prayers. The ones where my husband and I can sit together and hear the children giggle from the next room. The ones where I'm woken in the middle of every night because a little one wants to sleep in my "nook." Let us look for the blessings, friends. We don't have forever, but we have right now. Let's make it enough.

Dear God, You bless those who are gentle. Help me to be slow to anger and to look at the heart of others instead of judging their actions.

Gentleness

When I think of gentleness, I think of how the birth of Jesus came about. Matthew 1:18–19 tells us, "Mary was pledged to be married to Joseph, but before they came together, she was found to be pregnant through the Holy Spirit. Because Joseph her husband was faithful to the law, and yet did not want to expose her to public disgrace, he had in mind to divorce her quietly." Gentleness. He must have thought she was lying, and I'm sure he felt hurt and betrayed. Can you imagine the gossip in their small village when it appeared that she had conceived illegitimately? He could have had her stoned for such a transgression. When the angel told him that Mary was telling the truth, and he was to take her into his home and name the baby Jesus, Joseph had total faith. Like Mary, he said *yes* to the task God placed before them. He believed God's plan and honored and trusted his betrothed. Gentleness.

In the movie *The Nativity*, Joseph feeds his last piece of bread to the donkey so it won't grow weak and stumble with Mary. He falls asleep at the side of a river, and Mary washes the blood from his blistered feet. Tears run down their cheeks when they hold Jesus for the first time. Gentleness.

Philippians 4:5 says, "Let your gentleness be evident to all. The Lord is near." Is our gentleness evident to *all*? How can we do gentleness better today?

self-control

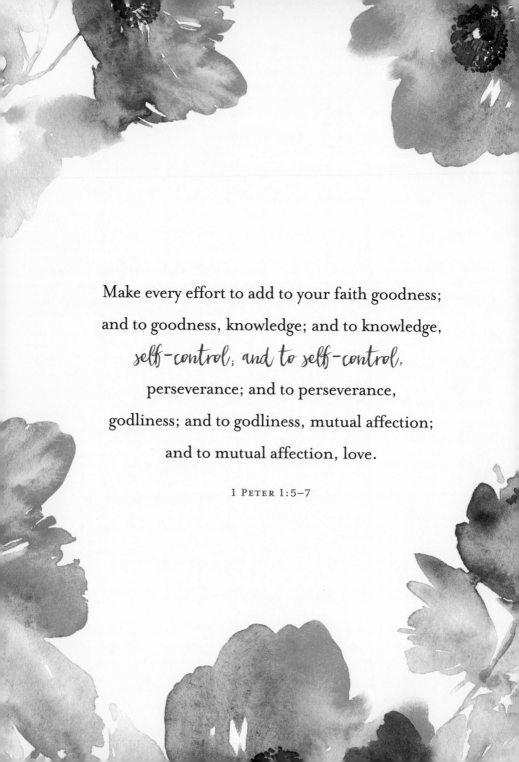

Make every effort to add to your faith goodness;
and to goodness, knowledge; and to knowledge,
self-control; and to self-control,
perseverance; and to perseverance,
godliness; and to godliness, mutual affection;
and to mutual affection, love.

1 PETER 1:5–7

The Importance of Listening

And a little child will lead them.
ISAIAH 11:6

There is a difference between hearing and listening. We can hear something without really listening to it. At any given moment, there are a dozen background noises that we tune out. However, if we concentrate and listen, we can name where each noise is coming from. It's the refrigerator humming. Or the neighbor's dog barking. Or a distant airplane. When we listen to what we are hearing, each of those background noises has meaning.

Have you ever heard someone talking but not really listened to what they have to say? I have. I'm especially guilty of it when one of my teenagers starts trying to convince me to let them do something new. Sometimes I'm *so sure* that I'm right and they are wrong that I tune them out before they even start talking. I'm half listening while I'm cleaning off the counter and making a grocery list in my head. I've already decided the answer is no before I have even heard what they have to say. My actions tell them that their words are not important. When I really listen to them, they usually have good ideas that I had not even considered. It takes a lot of self-control for me to surrender the fact that I no longer need to make every decision for them. They are doing what I taught them to do. They are being independent. They have their own friends, their own thoughts, ideas, and dreams. Many times those ideas are very different than mine, but that does not mean they are wrong. Their ideas and words are so very important. *We have to be careful not to make someone else's important words our background noise.*

I have a photo of my son Joshua when he was about a year and a half old. He had both of his hands on my cheeks, turning my head to look at him. He did that a lot, because he was smart enough to know that eye contact meant we were listening. Sometimes small children are such great teachers! Many of our circumstances can have different outcomes if we follow the lead of that small child and turn to look at someone when they speak to us. Make eye contact. Listen to what they have to say and weigh it carefully before we respond.

When we really listen, we hear the truth.

When we really listen, we see the pain or excitement behind their eyes.

When we really listen, we let them know they are important.

When we really listen, we open up lines of communication.

When we really listen, we allow them to trust us.

When we really listen, we build bridges instead of walls.

When we really listen, we validate their feelings.

When we feel we are heard, we speak the truth.

When we feel we are heard, we allow others to feel our pain or excitement.

When we feel we are heard, we feel important.

When we feel we are heard, we communicate more freely.

When we feel we are heard, we trust that person with our words and feelings.

When we feel we are heard, walls that were built between us start to crumble.

When we feel we are heard, we feel validated.

Dear Lord, I have to confess that sometimes I act as if I know the answer better than You do because I try to control every situation without talking to You first. Help me to remember that Your ways are better than my ways. Help me hear Your voice and seek Your counsel before I give a response to others.

The Happiest Place on Earth

Set a guard, over my mouth, LORD;
keep watch over the door of my lips.
PSALM 141:3

I'm guilty of it. I've seen a parent snap in the store and start yelling at their kid and thought, *Wow. If it's that bad right here in front of God and everybody, I'd hate to see what it's like at home.* But then we went to Disney. After standing in line in the rain for an hour waiting to enter the park, and after walking around on hot blacktop with a headache, one of my children wandered away from me and caused a frantic search. This particular child also refused to bring their sunglasses, then threw a tantrum because I wouldn't spend forty dollars in the souvenir shop to buy a new pair. This child had just gotten to go swimming, eaten ice cream with lunch, bought a new shirt, and chosen the last two rides, then complained for two hours because we were spending the day in Animal Kingdom instead of Magic Kingdom. I asked my child to please just stay next to me for the hundredth time, only to have them purposely lag behind and laugh. I snapped. I found myself yelling just like that parent in the store. I yelled something that resembled that scene where Chevy Chase flipped out in *National Lampoon's Vacation*.

Right about that time, a woman (with no children nagging her) walked past and glared at me and said to her friend, "Whoever said Disney was the happiest place on earth was lying." Wow. At first I was really mad about that comment. Just let her try to put up with what

I was listening to all morning and see how she would react! But after I'd had a while to process what she said, I realized it was true. Yes, my child was acting spoiled and entitled and needed to be put in their place. However, I would never have spoken to them like that if I thought that woman—or anyone else—was listening. It was a real eye opener to me as a parent. If I knew I wouldn't speak to my child that way in front of other people, it wasn't okay to speak like that at all. Even if nobody else was listening, my child was. *My child was.*

We've likely all lost our patience and spoken too harshly to someone we care about. The truth is that when we speak that way, it usually doesn't even cause the other person to stop the behavior we didn't like in the first place. All it does is put them in a defensive mode, ready to fight back. However, if we speak gently and correct people out of love, the outcome could be much different. A little self-control can go a long way.

May we use softer words and think of how they will be heard in others' ears before we speak them. May we not be so quick to cast judgment on others. We don't know their story, or what heartache they may be facing in their lives. May we always keep in mind that we are always setting an example. That example could be a positive one or a negative one. At the end of the day, may we go to bed with no regrets.

In what areas of our lives could we practice more self-control?

Dear Lord, sometimes I get so caught up with the aggravations in life that I forget to look for the blessings. Forgive me when my human heart reacts before my spiritual heart thinks. Please soften my heart, put a guard over my mouth, and help me practice more self-control.

When Self-Pruning Is in Order

*For, before the harvest, when the blossom is gone and the flower
becomes a ripening grape, he will cut off the shoots with pruning knives,
and cut down and take away the spreading branches.*

ISAIAH 18:5

Trees are pruned when branches are dead, wounded, or diseased because they pose a risk to the rest of the tree. Left unattended, they could allow disease to spread. Much like the trees, sometimes we need to cut the "dead stuff" out of our own lives. I came across a post I wrote when I was struggling to keep my head above water as a single mom. I had a lot of pruning to do, and it took a great deal of self-control to find the blessings. Allow me to share:

Reflecting for a minute before I collapse. I started this day by saying how I was thankful for the little things and wishing everyone a blessed day. Then my day began.

Started the morning by having the pleasure of being part of one of the real joys of small town living, which is small town gossip. But, I am thankful to be surrounded by family and friends who love and support me and know the truth. For that, I am blessed.

Trip #1 to Children's Hospital with Benjamin: Found out the break in his arm was near the growth plate, so he got a cast for four more weeks and can't play in the baseball tournaments. BUT, at least it's the end of the season, and the cast is waterproof this summer. For that, we are blessed.

On the way home, something on the car broke. Missed my niece's birthday party. I have no idea how I'm going to get it fixed, but God will provide. In the meantime, He already provided me with wonderful friends who let me borrow their car, and my niece had a great party anyway. For that, I am blessed.

Trip #2 to Children's Hospital: As soon as I got home, I had to go back with Emily, who had terrible tummy trouble. Was scared for a while, but all is well. Thank you to my amazing family and friends who knew and prayed, offered your help, support, and encouraging words. For you, I am blessed.

Just got home at 1:30 am, and while trying to open the door, put my hand on a spider the size of a mouse. But I have this beautiful house on this beautiful farm that my children love to come home to. For that I am blessed.

Today was a horrible day, but the blessings that bring joy were still there. Just not in the ways I thought. I'm glad my eyes were opened to them before I end my day so I can go to bed with a thankful heart.

Be joyful ALWAYS. Pray without ceasing. Give thanks in ALL circumstances. For this is God's will for you in Christ Jesus. 1 Thess. 5:16–18

What kinds of things are posing a risk to our physical and spiritual well-being? What are we leaving unattended that is threatening to spread to the part of us that keeps us alive and well-rounded and beautiful?

Dear Lord, thank You for showing me that Your goodness knows no bounds. Help me prune off the ugly parts of my nature and leave room for virtue to grow. Help me cut out the sadness, self-criticism, and unforgiveness and let the Son nourish and strengthen my soul.

Turn Away and Pray

My Facebook post on August 25, 2009, said, "I'm reprimanding myself ahead of time for eating the entire pizza I just put in the oven." That was even one of those rare summers when I wasn't pregnant! I was lacking a bit of self-control. Stifling our cravings is hard enough, but it's even more difficult to be in control of our emotions. Anxiety. Anger. Passion. Shame. Embarrassment. Loneliness. Fear. They seem to creep into our lives uninvited and set up camp. So how do we get them to pull the stakes and move along?

God knew that our lives would be full of temptations. Jesus Himself was tempted by Satan. Thankfully, 1 Corinthians 10:13 tells us that "no temptation has overtaken you except what is common to mankind. And God is faithful; he will not let you be tempted beyond what you can bear. But when you are tempted, he will also provide a way out so that you can endure it." Do you know how Jesus resisted the temptation? In Matthew 4, Jesus fasted and prayed. Then He said, "Away from me, Satan! For it is written: 'Worship the Lord your God, and serve him only'" (verse 10). He exercised self-control by turning His focus away from the temptation and onto God.

Are there any areas of your life where you wished you had better self-control? Have you offered them up in prayer? Please consider taking a moment to ask God to change your focus and to help you resist temptations.

Before You Start Your Day...

It's important to spend our time forming strong bonds with our family and friends, but it's also important to *be purposeful* about how we spend our time to form a strong bond with God. The Bible tells us more about how God wants us to spend our time. Ask God to help you use your time wisely as you study the following Scripture verses.

Spend time in *prayer*.

But when you pray, go into your room, close the door and pray to your Father, who is unseen. Then your Father, who sees what is done in secret, will reward you.

MATTHEW 6:6

Make time to *study* the word.

For everything that was written in the past was written to teach us, so that through the endurance taught in the Scriptures and the encouragement they provide we might have hope.

ROMANS 15:4

I meditate on your precepts and consider your ways. I delight in your decrees; I will not neglect your word.

PSALM 119:15–16

Spend time *giving* to others.

Therefore, as we have opportunity, let us do good to all people,
especially to those who belong to the family of believers.

GALATIANS 6:10

Spend time in *fellowship*:

And let us consider how we may spur one another on toward love and good deeds,
not giving up meeting together, as some are in the habit of doing,
but encouraging one another—and all the more as you see the Day approaching.

HEBREWS 10:24–25

Make time to *grow in knowledge*.

But grow in the grace and knowledge of our Lord and Savior Jesus Christ.
To him be glory both now and forever! Amen.

2 PETER 3:18

My Favorite Verses

Notes

Photo: Christian Dohn

About the author:

Denaé Jones graduated from Morehead State University with a degree in education. After teaching children with special needs for six years, she resigned to homeschool her own children. She currently works as a financial planner and writes a column for local newspapers. Her writing has previously been published in two of the *Chicken Soup for the Soul* books. She lives in Bethel, Ohio, with her husband and six children.

IF YOU ENJOYED THIS BOOK, WILL YOU CONSIDER SHARING THE MESSAGE WITH OTHERS?

Mention the book in a blog post or through Facebook, Twitter, Pinterest, or upload a picture through Instagram.

Recommend this book to those in your small group, book club, workplace, and classes.

Head over to Facebook at fb.me/EllieClaireGifts to "LIKE" the page, and post a comment as to what you enjoyed the most.

Tweet "I recommend reading #LoveJoyPeace by Denaé Jones // #inspiredbylife #devotions #ellieclairegifts

Pick up a copy for someone you know who would be challenged and encouraged by this message.

Write a review online.

Visit us online at EllieClaire.com

fb.me/EllieClaireGifts

Thank you.